The Culworth Gang

Richard Blacklee

Text Copyright © Richard Blacklee 2021
Richard Blacklee has asserted his right in accordance with the Copyright Designs and Patents Act 1988 to be identified as the author of this work.

All rights reserved.

No part of this publication may be lent, resold, hired out or reproduced in any form or by any means without prior written permission from the author and publisher. All rights reserved.

Copyright © 3P Publishing

First published in 2021 in the UK

3P Publishing
C E C, London Road
Corby
NN17 5EU

A catalogue number for this book is available from the British Library

ISBN 978-1-913740-23-8

Cover design: James Mossop

Highwayman: Tony Rotherham

Contents

Chapter One — 1
Introduction

Chapter Two — 3
Culworth Village

Chapter Three — 7
Highwaymen: Social Background

Chapter Four — 13
The Formation of the Culworth Gang

Chapter Five — 18
The Culworth Gang: Operations

Chapter Six — 23
The Arrests and Confessions

Chapter Seven — 28
The Summer Assizes of 1787

Chapter Eight — 31
The Gang's Final Letters

Chapter Nine — 35
The Hangings

Chapter Ten — 38
The Aftermath of the Hangings

Chapter Eleven — 40
Close to the Wind

Chapter Twelve — 42
Final Thoughts

Appendix — 46

Acknowledgements — 49

Bibliography — 56

Author notes — 57

Chapter One
Introduction

Four highwaymen were hung from the gallows at Northampton Racecourse on 3rd August 1787. The men were members of the Culworth Gang and their executions were watched by a huge crowd of over 5,000 people.

The breakup of the gang came shortly after two men from the Culworth area were arrested. They had been kept under discreet surveillance by a local constable after a vigilant inn keeper in Towcester noticed smock coats and black masks in their bags. The perpetrators of numerous and widely reported crimes in the area were known to wear such apparel and there were generous rewards being offered for information leading to convictions. When reports were received of a night-time burglary at nearby Blakesley, the suspects were taken to Northampton for questioning. The two men's confessions extracted at the County gaol led to a posse of lawmen raiding addresses in and around Culworth.

Surprisingly little has been written about the Culworth Gang considering they terrorised South Northamptonshire, Oxfordshire and neighbouring counties for around twenty years. Contemporary newspaper reports described the occupation of the majority of the men as labourers, although their recorded exploits suggest that some at least must have been skilled horsemen. Who were they, how did they evade capture for so many years, and why did their eventual hangings attract such a large crowd? This book seeks to answer some of the questions about the notorious Culworth Gang of Northamptonshire.

Chapter Two
Culworth Village

The village and parish of Culworth was known in early records as Coleworth or Culeworth pronounced Cul'uth (as in pull'uth). The name comes from Cula, a man's name, and worth, meaning an enclosure or settlement.

Culworth is located south of the A5 Watling Street in south western Northamptonshire, about seven miles from Banbury and close to the Oxfordshire and Warwickshire borders. A very long time ago Watling Street was the recognised boundary between the Danes and the Saxons. The lands to the north were Viking territory known as the Danelaw, the lands to the south were ruled by the Saxons. The Culworth Gang were similarly territorial, keeping mostly to their southern side of Watling Street. The Roman built road has traditionally been likened to a tribal boundary, and even until the 1960s local people could frequently distinguish which side of Watling Street someone came from by their accent. Rev T Mozley, in his 'Reminiscences of life in South Northamptonshire in the early nineteenth century' wrote that its wild and native character had a certain charm. Dave Hewitt of Bugbrooke History Group, who has considerably assisted the author with his freely shared knowledge of the days of the Culworth Gang, likens the lawlessness of eighteenth-century Northamptonshire south of Watling Street to the 'Wild West'.

Located at the very heart of England, two ancient droveways or drifts crossed at Culworth, the Welsh Road (Anglesey to London) and Banbury Lane (Mid Wales to Northampton). These drovers' tracks were used for taking livestock from hill country in Wales to fattening ground and markets in the Midlands and South East. Lengths of the old routes survive as modern roads although other sections are now unsurfaced byways. These quiet lanes would have been useful to the highwaymen during their clandestine outings.

Culworth is sited on a hilltop close to the source of a tributary of the river Cherwell. This river, the northernmost Thames tributary, was formerly known as the Charwelle, and is frequently still pronounced as such. The Cherwell at Banbury formed the county boundary between Northamptonshire and Oxfordshire prior to boundary reorganisation in the twentieth century. Before land drainage schemes were implemented the Cherwell presented a far more formidable barrier than the gentle brook seen near Culworth today. The fords and narrow bridges crossing the river at Slat Mill, Cropredy, Hay's Bridge and Trafford Bridge caused bottlenecks for travellers, tradesmen and livestock droves alike, and particularly for large armies on the move. There were major military engagements on Danes Moor below Culworth during the times of the Danes and the Saxons, the War of the Roses, and the English Civil War. King Charles 1 is said to have spent the night at Culworth Manor House on the eve of the Battle of Edgehill in 1642. Two years later he was back in the area for the Battle of Cropredy Bridge. This time he is reported to have stayed in a poor man's house at Williamscot, Wardington, as there was a smallpox outbreak at the big house.

***

At the time of the Culworth Gang's activities in the late eighteenth century, the village was largely self-sufficient. The 1777 Militia List records village men working as bakers, blacksmiths, butchers, carpenters, chairmakers, cordwainers (shoemakers), farmers, graziers, grocers, labourers, millers, servants and tailors. The village is likely to have had lace makers, for the families of agricultural workers often supplemented their income 'working at the lace'. Northamptonshire was also an important wool producing county and many villages provided combers, knitters and weavers.

From this description, eighteenth century Culworth might sound like an idyllic place to have lived, offering numerous and varied employment opportunities. Inevitably, it wasn't quite as simple as that, as the writings of Rev Mozley explain. There were many paupers who didn't fit the above job descriptions and everyone had to be given something to do in return for parish poor payments. The rate payers of the village would meet in the pub once a month to share out jobs for those who would otherwise be unemployed. It was known as the 'monthly apportionment of the paupers'. The gentlemen of the village would always find paupers something to do, however menial or unnecessary the tasks might be. Reverend Mozley says there were some forty paupers in his previous parish of Deddington. They spent their days doing very little work indeed in the stone quarry, but at least it occupied their time. The paupers were mostly men, for women and girls worked at the lace from around the age of five. This kept the girls from playing outside in the mud and dirtying their dresses. Schooling lasted only till the ages of ten or eleven and Rev Mosely commented that the ignorance of the young village people was lamentable. Many children were dressed in rags, often half naked and shoeless. Sometimes village women were ashamed to attend church, or even to leave their homes, for they were so poorly dressed. Lady Dryden of Canon's Ashby would do what she could to help, and there was often a queue outside her door of those seeking charity or perhaps an old pair of shoes.

Times were extremely hard for the majority of the population, and there was widespread discontent and social unrest in the country.

***

With the steady introduction of industrialisation throughout England, major improvements were required to the transport infrastructure. Turnpikes were introduced on busy roads in an attempt to try to recoup some of the costs of road construction and maintenance. There were a number of turnpike trusts in Northamptonshire, and the nearby Watling Street, a former drove road, had toll houses every few miles. Whichever direction one took from Culworth village one soon come across a turnpike, known locally as a 'great road'. To the west there was the Banbury to Daventry, to the north east the Daventry to Towcester (Watling Street), to the southeast the Brackley to Towcester, and to the south the Banbury to Brackley turnpike roads.

As it was mainly the better off who could afford the tolls to travel on these great roads, passengers in coaches or those on horseback or on foot made tempting targets for robbery. Of course, great care needed to be taken by highwaymen when robbing on the turnpikes.

The roads were often fenced, with the ends of each section blocked by a pike barrier. The turnpike was a long pole fitted with vicious horizontal pikes which spanned the highway, swivelling around a central pivot. Once the toll had been paid the pole was rotated to allow travellers to pass, one by one. The barrier inhibited quick escape for highwaymen when pursued, so they had to pick hold-up places with care. Although turnpikes tended to be better maintained than minor roads, they were still often deeply rutted, and overturned carriages were a daily occurrence. Frequently, coaches were only able to proceed at a fast-walking pace. Heavy goods trucks such as those carrying coal into the county were able to use the roads only when they were dry.

The proximity of the turnpike roads was fundamental to the success of the Culworth Gang, offering rich pickings within easy reach of their homes. The ancient byways and green ways traversing the village provided quiet and convenient access in all directions to and from the turnpikes. The mobility of the gang was therefore not compromised to any great degree by the recent introduction of enclosure of the open fields with fencing, walls and hedges. Tribes of gipsies caused a bit of a nuisance by camping on the byways and keeping farmers in continual terror. Rev Mozely wrote that one well-known local gypsy character called Nehemiah Smith went about with over forty horses.

Chapter Three
Highwaymen: Social Background

The English Civil War of 1642–51 and the Restoration of the monarchy in 1660 led to a golden period for 'knights of the road'. Many of the early highwaymen and women came from privileged landowning backgrounds, from wealthy families whose estates had been destroyed during the fighting or sequestered by the victorious parliamentarians. A large number of families suffered further catastrophic loss of money and property as a result of the South Sea Bubble collapse in 1720. Many never recovered financially, adding to the country's economic problems and heightened social tensions.

From the late 16th century to the end of the eighteenth, Northamptonshire held the seat of two ducal families, a marquis, thirteen earls, two barons and five baronets. The area south of Watling Street was known as the land of great squires and fine country estates. The three towns of Brackley, Daventry and Towcester remained relatively free from the encroach of industry. The period after the Restoration was a time for conservative remodelling. The fine Northamptonshire houses were generally tastefully restored, rather than replaced with new. A number of county families restored their fortunes in the Indies, from sugar and rum plantations in Jamaica and Antigua.

***

Rural communities depended largely upon their rights of access to open fields in order to survive. Open fields had been ploughed by oxen since medieval times, creating a distinctive ridge and furrow effect on the landscape, sometimes with strips many miles in length. These can still be seen in places, criss-crossed by walls and hedges from enclosure. By the time of the first census in 1801, Culworth had 110 houses and 531 inhabitants. England as a whole had a population of nine million. A hundred years earlier the population was calculated to have been five and a half million. Ways had to be found to feed the rapidly increasing population. Enclosures heralded the beginning of more efficient farming methods, but inevitably to the detriment of the common man.

George III, who ascended the throne in 1760, was affectionately known as 'Farmer George'. He took a keen interest in agriculture and was all in favour of increasing production to feed the growing masses. In order to make their agricultural estates more efficient and thereby profitable, the major landowners could present a bill before Parliament for the appointment of commissioners to oversee enclosure. The commissioners, often local gentlemen or esquires and practical farmers themselves, were responsible for setting out the boundaries for fields and roadways, footpaths and bridleways, etc. Many villagers consequently lost their ancient rights to farm open fields and 'wastes'. Wastes were the moors, fens, wetlands, rocky ground, etc, over which villagers enjoyed collective rights of access for grazing their animals and collecting hay crops and wood, and catching fish. Vast areas of heavy clay farmland were drained to increase crop production and yield. Clay ware pipes were manufactured in local estate brickyards, using material freely available. Draining the land did not meet with universal approval for the sweetest butter was produced from dairy cattle grazing where the 'grips were foul,' the flooded hollows in in the fields where the grass was finest. When cattle were kept in stalls and their manure collected and spread, the nitrogen levels in the fields increased.

The commissioners allocated land for stone quarries for road building. However, many roads became virtually impassable after the enclosures when insufficient stone, sand and gravel was made available for maintenance. Rev Mozely wrote of encountering ruts half a yard deep.

Land owners or proprietors were responsible for the cost of enclosing the yardlands (about thirty acres), quarterns, and sixteenths they were awarded by the commissioners. Enclosure was typically by timber post and rail fencing, hedging with hawthorn quicksets and sometimes by drystone walls when local stone was freely available. In addition to the cost of the materials, there was the price of labour for enclosing the land. Land awarded was generally considered poor compensation by villagers for losing their former grazing rights over extensive areas of common land. Clashes were frequent when newly erected fencing was torn down. A major part of the commissioners' remit was to settle the numerous disputes which arose. In an attempt to avoid criticism that only the wealthy benefited from enclosure, a small area of land might be set aside for the exercise and recreation of the people.

It appeared to many that the rich were again soon living in splendour after the Civil War, the poor still dying in squalor, and the gap was widening. The average age of death in the eighteenth century was around thirty-six, and parish officers were reputedly known to starve poor children so they would not live to become a burden on the community.

It was against this depressing economic background that a new lower class of highwayman emerged.

***

An example of a local highwayman from a modest background was James Hind from Chipping Norton in Oxfordshire, about twenty miles from Culworth. James was a butcher, his father a saddler. James enlisted with alacrity into the king's army to fight for the Royalist Stuart cause. After his beloved monarch Charles I was executed in 1649, James Hind undertook a personal campaign against leading parliamentarians. He became a serious threat to those he despised the most for regicide, whilst at the same time becoming the darling of the many who supported his cause. Well known for his chivalry, James Hind became a kind of Robin Hood figure, robbing the rich and feeding the poor. As the penalty for theft was the same at either end of the scale, Hind chose mostly the top end for his exploits. It is said he even successfully robbed Oliver Cromwell himself.

Of course, like most highwaymen, Hind's luck eventually ran out. He was condemned to the barbarous fate of drawing, hanging and quartering at Worcester in 1652. This was a highly ritualised procedure of dragging the condemned to the place of execution where, after hanging, the body was disembowelled, beheaded, burnt and quartered. The head and body parts were often put on public display.

Due to his popularity no one could be found to speak against Hind as a highwayman. The parliamentarians instead accused him of being a traitor. This was on the grounds he had continued his open support for the Stuart cause even after the execution of Charles I. When Charles II was returned to the throne in 1660 he ensured the same grisly fate of drawing, hanging and quartering befell his father's executioners, the parliamentary soldiers Francis Hacker and Daniel Axtell.

James Hind became a legend in his own lifetime and a role model for future generations of highwaymen, although few who came after him were as gentlemanly towards their victims.

Most highwaymen operated around London, where robbery on the highway was a daily event. The hazardous nature of the work usually made it a short-lived career. Young highwaymen were prone to over excitement, commonly assaulting their male victims and abusing the females. They frequently discharged their single shot flintlock pistols in error, enabling potential victims to fight back. Many a highwayman was shot in the back as they turned away. A young highwayman's money was typically soon spent on drinking, womanising and gambling, before he returned to the roads to commit further robberies until eventually his luck ran out.

***

England considered itself a relatively free country compared with continental Europe where military regimes swiftly put paid to any highwayman activity. Indeed, England had no centralised law enforcement agency throughout the whole of the eighteenth century. It wasn't until the Gordon Riots in 1780, when over 400 mostly gin sodden rioting Londoners were killed that serious consideration was given to establishing a professional police force. Instead, in the countryside in particular, it was left to the initiative of parishes and hundreds (a hundred being a subdivision of a shire – Culworth is in Sutton hundred) to appoint constables. They were said to be men with a sense of civic duty, although, to be fair, there were fringe benefits such as being exempt from certain taxes. The High Constable was typically an important and powerful figure, perhaps a landowner or member of the clergy, able to pay under-constables to do the dirty work. A constable was sometimes an unpaid position, relying on financial rewards from the beneficiaries of their services. Constables would be assisted as the need arose by volunteers and vigilante groups, on occasion using bloodhounds for tracking miscreants. Local manorial authorities were described in the writings of Rev Mozley as quite inaccessible if not also utterly powerless. They did little other than hold court once a year at which officers were appointed and trifling quit rents received.

Without effective law enforcement in England robbery was a major problem. Victims who could afford it relied on advertising their losses and encouraging informers. Extremely generous rewards were offered to thief-takers and others to catch criminals and recover stolen goods. There was no shortage of willing volunteers when the rewards for success were so high.

From around 1744 magistrates were paid, and it was one of these, Justice the Rev Michael O'Clare of Maidford about six miles to the north east of the village, who was largely instrumental in ending the reign of the Culworth Gang. Rev O'Clare was related to Gilbert de Clare, 7th Earl of Gloucester, known as the Red Earl because of his red hair and fiery temper in battle. Rev Michael seems to have inherited his relative's temperament, if not his wealth. There is a train of thought that the reverend relentlessly pursued the Culworth gang for the reward money on offer. Perhaps he needed the income to maintain his lavish lifestyle, and to keep up with his peers in their fine country houses.

Wealthy clergymen living in their grand rectories and dispensing harsh justice to the common people were sometimes deeply despised. Not all churchgoers agreed with the rites and ceremonies prescribed in the Anglican Book of Common Prayer. Ordinary people increasingly supported independent chapels and simpler services advocated by the likes of Rev Richard Davis of Rothwell, known as the apostle of Northamptonshire.

After the gang members were identified in April 1787 Rev O'Clare advertised for victims of robberies to make themselves known to him. He wished to compile the most damning case possible to ensure capital convictions. In some quarters this victimisation was not popularly received. Parish records show Rev O'Clare ruffled quite a few feathers whilst incumbent at Maidford, from 1772 until his death in 1798.

Chapter Four
The Formation of the Culworth Gang

By the late eighteenth century, the work of enclosing farm land was proceeding apace, leading to a huge increase in the number of thefts and assaults by desperate citizens turning to crime.

By the time the Culworth Gang commenced their activities around 1765, around a third to one half of small-time farmers had been forced off the open fields and wastes by enclosure. Options for the displaced were limited. They could seek employment as labourers for the new owners of their traditional lands. They could move into the towns (although the Industrial Revolution was replacing many workers by machines, and fierce competition for available jobs was pushing down wages). They could emigrate to the New World that was opening up, or they could turn to crime. A hundred and fifty years after the end of the Civil War, Culworth had become largely forgotten. The village had been bypassed by the turnpikes, and its presence even omitted from small-scale maps. It was probably a case of out of sight out of mind until John Smith and his confederates decided to adopt the desperate option of turning to crime.

Described as a labourer, and a man 'of great bodily strength and daring energy of character', Smith was born in 1734. He lived at Culworth for twenty-six years after his marriage to Elizabeth Tack in November 1761. This was a year destined to be remembered for a century or more as the driest on record, the year the cattle died for the want of both water and grass. It was hardly an auspicious start to married life for the Smiths.

John and Elizabeth Smith had at least four children: William, born in 1762, John Jnr, born in 1763, another son Benjamin and a daughter, Molly. It has been suggested Smith turned to crime because he lacked the skills or inclination to earn a living by honest means. Perhaps, although he was only one of very many people at the time who were forced to steal the commodities they needed for their daily lives. A stolen cotton pocket handkerchief could be sold for sixpence, whereas a lace handkerchief might fetch six shillings, and feed a family for a month. Clothing required a large part of a family's budget after food. It was incredibly rare, perhaps unique, for more than one member of a family to be present at a highway robbery because of the danger. The Smiths are recorded as having two or more of the family at the scene of some of their crimes.

Another gang member, William Pettifer, was born locally in 1747. Some reports say he came from Paulerspury, others from Charlton by Newbottle, or Farthinghoe, but they are all reasonably close to Culworth. Pettifer used the alias Peckover, although there is a train of thought that Pettifer was a pseudonym for Peckover and not the other way around, or perhaps the names were interchangeable. Either way, there are still distant relatives of the man living in Northamptonshire with both spellings. Annette Taylor, née Cooknell, is from a family associated with the gang from when the Cooknells resided at Hangland Farm. Annette told the author she believes the Peckovers lived at the nearby Fernhill Farm in the 1780s and she confirms the story that some gang members are thought to have hidden in the barn around the time of the arrests in 1787.

According to an entry in WikiTree, William Pettifer was married twice in Culworth church, in 1766 and 1768 (his first wife died), and he had a son and five daughters. The witnesses who signed the register were Rich Yates and Elizabeth Thornton at the first ceremony and Thomas Needle and Jane Thornton at the second. It is possible these girls were relatives of a nearby landed gentry family, the Thorntons of Brockhall who provided the county with High Sheriffs in 1672 and 1698. A relative of another leading gang member, William Bowers, by the name of Richard Bowers (1790-1856) was married into the Thornton family around 1815-18 when he married another Elizabeth, only a few years after the executions. It is therefore perhaps plausible some of the gang might not have been from such humble backgrounds as is generally assumed. The gang members who were executed were given a decent Christian burial in Anglian churchyards, whereas other highwaymen's bodies had sometimes been simply left to rot on gibbets by the side of the road.

Another gang member, William Abbot, shoemaker, and the flamboyant Clerk of Sulgrave Parish, reputedly carried loaded pistols about his person wherever he went, even during his sacred churchly duties. Although this might sound unlikely, it could be true. He might as well have carried weapons, for the penalty for being caught in possession of a firearm was no worse than for stealing a lace handkerchief for instance: the sentence of death.

Very few personal details are known about any of the other gang members other than names recorded in the local papers. Any court records appear long since lost. It is known the gang numbered at least fifteen members at their peak. It has long been suggested there may have been a mastermind behind the activities of the Culworth Gang, a so-called Mr Big, but if so then his or her identity remains a mystery.

The Culworth Gang are reputed to have meticulously planned their robberies at a number of public houses and remote barns in the area. The Red Lion at Culworth, the Star Inn at Sulgrave, the Gaydon Inn, Job's barn at Warden Hill and the barn at Fernhill Farm on Thorpe Hill have all been mentioned as likely meeting places. Certainly, the landlords of local hostelries are likely to have been aware of the identity of the gang members, and perhaps basked in the notoriety. Village lads from ten years upwards were typically recruited to act as informers. The boys would watch the comings and goings of travellers at local inns and provide the gang with information about those undertaking journeys through their patch.

The Culworth Gang were known for being of particularly fierce disposition and to intimidate their victims. Certainly, highwaymen needed to be of forceful character to persuade their victims to obey orders without question or delay. Horses and weapons could be hired, bought or, alternatively, borrowed or stolen. The gang are known to have used horses, for they are described in contemporary newspaper reports as highwaymen rather than footpads. They must have possessed the wherewithal for stabling horses. Rev O'Clare's notice in the *Northampton Mercury* of 23rd June 1787 refers to the 'instruments of death in their hands'. Weapons of choice included the flintlock pistol and blunderbuss, with their horn of powder and a bag of bullets. Billy clubs, a sword or scimitar, and even a pitchfork are known to have been used by robbers.

From the descriptions of the recorded robberies, it is clear the gang members worked together as a team, mostly two or three at a time, with up to seven in the case of the hold-up of Mr Richardson the Oxford carrier. It certainly took valour to stick a pistol into a darkened carriage not knowing what the reaction would be from the occupants. For that reason, a mild moonlit night was the most popular time for a hold-up, for highwaymen couldn't see what they were doing if it was too dark and the roads themselves were treacherous. There was little sympathy expressed for travellers foolish enough to travel at night. Parishes and hundreds were responsible for reimbursing victims of crimes on the highway during daytime but not at night. Constables would be keen to identify criminals stealing during daylight hours whereas less heed would be taken of robbers operating after dusk.

By choice, highwaymen favoured stealing currency, jewellery and expensive cloth, which didn't weigh too much to carry away. Many items considered low value today were also highly prized by house robbers. Lead and cast-iron goods, clothing, pots and pans, spoons and forks, etc, which could be easily sold at local markets were frequently stolen.

***

The English Militia was a force raised for the defence of the realm against invasion or rebellion. The Lord Lieutenant of Northamptonshire was required to nominate 640 able-bodied men between the ages of eighteen and forty-five from a list of 13,741 names. Poor men and married men with three or more children were usually exempt from the ballot. The recruits were trained and exercised for twenty-eight days annually. This might account for at least four Culworth Gang members shown in the 1777 Militia List being skilled horsemen. The four names are William Smith, Richard Law and William Tyrell of Culworth, and William Abbot of Sulgrave. The highwaymen covered considerable distances on occasion. They must have been experienced riders in order to spend hours in the saddle in all weathers, always wary, and ready to gallop away if pursued. Another name on the Militia List for Culworth is Thomas Thornton, butcher. The name Thornton crops up quite a lot in connection with the gang, and, although complete speculation on the part of the author, it is just possible the robbers had an amenable local butcher to process the livestock they stole. Surely, they would have needed a skilled butcher to take in the whole carcasses of lamb, pig and sides of beef, and break them down into primal cuts, without enquiring too closely from whence they came?

Chapter Five
The Culworth Gang: Operations

The Culworth Gang started modestly enough. Perhaps half a dozen villagers came together under the direction of John Smith to trap deer and game, exercising what had traditionally been a customary right. The men wore smocks and blackened their faces, copying the example of well-known gangs of English poachers. Although the meat was for the personal consumption of the men and their families, poaching was one of the named capital offences under the Black Act of 1723. They could not afford to be caught. Over the years the list of capital offences was expanded to include over 200 capital crimes, whereas the legal rights of defendants remained strictly limited.

As the gang grew in numbers, their activities widened to include burglary, sheep and cattle rustling, and highway robbery. South Northamptonshire hostelries abounded with tales of feloniously sinister figures in smocks and masks who roamed the highways at night. The remote rural location of Culworth and its proximity to byways and turnpikes made the village an ideal base for these activities. There were numerous fairs and markets in the area, advertised weekly in the local paper the *Mercury*. Traders and farmers with bulging wallets passed close to Culworth. The busy section of turnpike between Brackley and Towcester traversed Whittlebury Forest, taking coaches and goods carts between Oxford and Northampton. These offered potentially rich rewards for vigilant robbers lying in wait.

The majority of the gang's recorded robberies were carried out to the east of the Oxford Canal which was under construction at the time of their operations. The river Cherwell and the adjacent canal workings provided formidable barriers for those travelling west of Wardington. The seventy-eight-mile-long Oxford canal was constructed between 1769-1790, and for fifteen years provided the main canal artery between the Midlands and London for heavy goods including stone and coal. The canal was built as cheaply as possible using many seasonal Irish farm labourers. They had experience of building drains with a spade with a stout narrow blade known as a draft. They learned the art of canal building as they went along. The official name for canals was the Inland Navigation System, and diggers were known as navigators, shortened to 'navvies'.

***

One of the Culworth Gang's most brutal recorded robberies was of Mr Wyatt, a Sulgrave farmer. Banging on his door in the middle of the night, pretending to be drovers seeking overnight refuge for their pigs, the gang set upon Mr Wyatt as soon as he stepped outside. After beating him up and locking him in the pantry with his wife, they stole goods to the value of £40. Mr Wyatt was 'stamped upon his breast whereby he was most shockingly bruised both on his head and inwardly'. This led to the owner of Stuchbury Hall on the Welsh Lane between Sulgrave and Helmdon setting a man trap behind his house, with iron bars across his shutters. Around this time the outlying Hangland Farmhouse was under construction between Thorpe Mandeville and Wardington. The stout oak beam securing the sole entrance door against the incursions of the Culworth Gang is still in use today.

In November 1783, the gang had a narrow escape during a robbery of the house of Mr Eaglestone in Old Wolverton, some twenty miles from Culworth. Accosting a servant leaving the property, they threatened to kill him if he didn't let them into the house. On entering the house, they were set upon by Mr Eaglestone and his other servants, and very nearly apprehended. During the struggle, one of the servants knocked out a colleague by mistake, allowing the robbers a brief opportunity to make good their escape.

John Smith, John Smith Jnr, William Smith, Pettifer, Tyrell, Bowers, and Law, robbed Mr. Richardson, the Oxford Carrier on the way to Northampton. About eight o'clock at night they stopped the wagon and one of the men stuck Richardson in the shoulder with a pitch-fork. They drove the cart behind a hedge some distance from the road. Two stood guard over Richardson and his son while the others ransacked 'all the loading', which took them three quarters of an hour. The robbers finally carried off money and goods to the value of a hundred and forty pounds.

**

The author is frequently asked how many gang members took part in the various robberies. The answer is that records show there were usually two or three, although in the case of the Oxford Carrier robbery there were seven robbers identified by name. There is more about the Richardson robbery in chapter six.

In March 1773 Tyrell, Bowers and Law robbed Hopper's-Ford toll-gate-house near Whitfield on the Brackley to Towcester turnpike. The trustees of the turnpike road offered a reward of ten guineas for information leading to a conviction. Ten guineas in 1773 was the equivalent of over £1,500 today, a huge reward.

Pettifer, John Smith the Elder and Tyrell robbed Elizabeth Thornton's house at Adson, Cropredy. The newspaper report says after confining Mrs Thornton to bed they robbed the house of about six pounds (nearly a year's pay for a labourer) together with 'wearing apparel to a considerable amount'. Whether this Elizabeth Thornton is the same lady who acted as a witness at William Pettifer's wedding at Culworth, or is connected to the Thorntons of Brockhall, or even the butcher called Thornton mentioned in chapter four, is not known.

The following story emphasises the gang's operational capabilities. In one single night members of the gang carried out a robbery in Towcester, another in Stony Stratford, and some cattle rustling at Brackley. They robbed a mail coach at Hopcroft's Holt and another coach near Gaydon Inn, followed by burglary of the inn itself. All these offences occurred during the same, no doubt very long, night!

**

Livestock driven down from hill country in springtime for fattening up in the Home Counties before slaughter for the London market must have offered a tempting target. However, there are no reports of the Culworth Gang attacking livestock droves. Perhaps this was because the valuable herds of store cattle and sheep, and flocks of geese and turkeys – often accompanied by boxes of cash -

were known to be shepherded by experienced drovers with working dogs, and protected by guards. The guards were frequently tough former military men armed with flintlocks and swords, and often fugitives from justice themselves. Many were deserters, for England was involved in wars with the Dutch and the French.

The maturity and experience of the Culworth Gang members is said to have contributed to their longevity. John Smith was in his thirties when he commenced operations, and fifty-three when he died. Most highwaymen who were executed were only in their twenties. Although undoubtedly violent in their actions, the gang were noted for leaving living witnesses to their robberies, which was not always the case with others. Despite the maxim 'Dead men tell no tales' and their reputation as abandoned ruffians, there is no record of anyone from the Culworth Gang ever killing anyone. They were extremely careful and cunning, enabling them to continue their activities for very many years without discovery. Several members had actually died before the gang were finally rounded up. Many people must have known of their activities, but it was thought they induced such fear in others that no one dared to come forward to denounce them.

Another theory is that the longevity of the gang was in part due to their support of the local poor. This view was put forward by the former headmaster of Byfield School, Mr Poole, who wrote in his 1930 book *History of Byfield* that members of the Culworth Gang nipped over to his nearby village at Christmas time in 1785 to steal some chickens! He believed one or more of the principals of the gang had connections in his village.

The Culworth Gang were perhaps revered by many ordinary folks, in much the same way as the highwaymen James Hind (chapter three) and Robin Hood. A lot of what they stole was edible, and it is thought they provided food to those in need, in return for their loyalty and silence. The crimes they committed might not have been justified, but a bit of extra food on the table was no doubt gratefully received.

Disguise was all important, and it was the Culworth Gang's frighteningly distinctive 'uniform' of faded fawn smocks, black hoods and masks that protected their identities for so long, but eventually contributed to their downfall.

Chapter Six
The Arrests and Confessions

The end of the Culworth Gang's long crime wave came after two of their number, Richard Law and William Pettifer, alias Peckover, were overheard bragging at a Towcester inn one evening. They told the landlord they had been 'a cocking at Blakesley that day' and that they were carrying gamecocks in their bags. As it was late and a journey of nearly thirteen miles over rough gated roads back to Culworth, the men arranged to stay the night. The landlord, Mr Duffin, inspected their bags after the men had retired, perhaps to check that the birds had sufficient food and water. He found two smock coats and a couple of face masks, but no fowl. Being aware that a local gang of robbers wore distinctive dress of farm labourers' smocks and had their faces blackened, Duffin summoned a constable. Duffin must have thought his luck was in for he would have been aware of the large rewards being offered for the conviction of felons. Many landlords of the time were noted rogues, so it is just as likely Duffin was searching the men's bags for something to steal.

The constable decided that, discretion being the better part of valour, he would do no more than to await further events for he 'had no doubt but some plan was in agitation'. A few days afterwards a report was received that the Mayo's farmhouse near Blakesley had been broken into. Mr Mayo and his wife were robbed of what little money they had, along with sundry articles of wearing apparel. The robbers were dressed in smock frocks and had their faces blacked. The landlord and the constable were able to provide information leading to the arrest of the two men who had stayed at the pub, which unfortunately hasn't yet been identified. Law and Pettifer were arrested and taken before a magistrate. A warrant was obtained for searching their houses and known hideouts, where great quantities of stolen goods were found. One hiding place was a vault beneath a local farm barn, although it is not recorded whether this was Fernhill barn, Job's barn or somewhere else. Rev O'Clare listed the items in the newspaper to encourage robbery sufferers to make themselves known to him 'to ensure such a daring gang might not possibly escape for want of prosecutors.'

On Monday 9th April 1787, Richard Law and William Pettifer were committed to Northampton County gaol by Justice Rev O'Clare. They were held pending trial at the Northampton Summer Assizes on the charge of 'breaking into the house of William Mayo and his wife at Sewell in the parish of Blakesley'. Despite vehemently protesting their innocence, the two men feared their chain of connection to fellow gang members whom they knew to be actually responsible for the Blakesley robbery, under the leadership of William Bowers, might lead to their capital conviction anyway.

Only two years earlier, an innocent man called James Tarry, or Tarvey, a labourer from Chipping Warden, had been hanged at Northampton (on 22nd July 1785) for the highway robbery of Mr William Adams near Chipping Warden. Messrs Law and Pettifer were well aware that the Adams robbery had in fact been carried out by John and William Smith and Thomas Malsbury. Mistaken identity was quite a frequent occurrence. This was a tragic miscarriage of justice as apart from being completely innocent Tarry left behind 'an honest faithful wife and three children'.

***

Rev Beesley's 1841 account says Law and Pettifer confessed after 'being strongly pressed'. This might refer to the barbaric torture whereby prisoners were stripped and laid spread-eagled on their backs on the floor of a low dark room in the prison. Wrists and ankles were stretched out and attached by cords to iron rings. Great weights of iron and stone were stacked on to their chests. The prisoner's diet, until either confessing or dying, was 'three morsels of the worst barley bread the first day, and if he lives beyond it he has nothing daily but as much foul water as he can drink'. It was specified the water should come from the puddle nearest to the cell door. If gaolers became impatient waiting for an obstinate malefactor to either confess or die, they would sometimes sit on the body to expedite suffocation.

Incorrectly assuming they were not suspected of being leading figures in the Culworth Gang and would be leniently treated if they cooperated, Law and Pettifer confessed their knowledge of thirty crimes committed by the gang (see the list in the appendix). They impeached the three Smiths, William Bowers, and several other gang members. The names published shortly afterwards in the *Northampton Mercury* were John Smith, his two sons William and John Jnr, William Bowers, William Abbot, Thomas Malsbury, William Tyrell and John Tack (possibly a cousin of the Smith boys, as their mother's maiden name was Tack).

Following Law and Pettifer's confessions, the constable and his assistants swooped on addresses in and around Culworth. They may very well have come the eight miles from Brackley market as implied in Stuart Marson's song 'Close to the Wind' (see Chapter Eleven) for Culworth lies in the administrative district of Brackley.

On Friday 13th April 1787 John Smith, William Smith and William Tyrell were formally charged. The initial sample charge was 'of being amongst a group of seven who robbed John Richardson the Northampton–Oxford carrier on 18th January 1785 at about 8pm at Sturdys Castle on the Oxford to Banbury turnpike [other reports say near Brackley], stealing money and goods to the value of £140'. Benjamin Smith, thought to be William and John Jnr's younger brother, was charged 'with receiving part of the said goods, knowing them to have been stolen'.

The *Oxford Mercury* reported the arrest of the men 'with pleasure' as Richardson came from Oxford. The newspaper reported 'the Villains drove his Cart under a Hedge some Distance from the Road and plundered it of Goods and Money to the Amount of One Hundred and Forty Pounds [equivalent to about £22,000 today]'. The 'proprietor', (presumably Richardson or his employer) made a public appeal in the *Mercury* for subscriptions in order to pay compensation to the passengers.

William Bowers was charged with stealing several pieces of velveret and other articles of the value of forty shillings and upwards, being the property of Mr James Rylance of Manchester. Elizabeth Tyrell (Bowers' girlfriend) was charged with stealing, receiving and concealing goods to the value of £5, the property of Mr Rylance, and others. Charles Dixon was charged with stealing, receiving and 'secreting divers' goods' of the value of forty shillings, the property of the said Mr Rylance.

A great quantity of stolen property was recovered during the raids, and the inventory made by Justice Rev Michael O'Clare, was published in an advertisement in the *Mercury*.

The advertisement columns of the *Northampton Mercury* frequently printed such announcements on behalf of 'Societies for the prosecution against all depredators on their property of robbers'. They requested information that might result in the arrest and conviction of those responsible for robberies and the recovery of stolen items. Justice Rev O'Clare was said to have been obsessive in his pursuit of the Culworth Gang, almost to the extent of having a vendetta against them. By all accounts he wasn't a very nice man and apparently was a bit of a rogue. He also listed the recovered items on hand bills. The high purchase price of the *Mercury* put it outside the affordability of the average commoner. More affordable penny broadsides or hand bills, and a halfpenny confessions sheet, were also printed by the *Mercury* to ensure news and announcements reached a wider readership.

William Abbot the shoemaker and Sulgrave Parish Clerk, also turned King's Evidence. He confessed his knowledge of a further seventeen crimes in which he and his confederates were concerned. This brought the total number of available charges against the suspects to at least forty-seven. Following William Abbot's confession, Sulgrave Church was closely searched, and a cache of stolen goods recovered from within the church chest.

***

The arrests would likely have caused serious repercussions for friends and relatives of those confined to Northampton County gaol, for they were expected to pay for a prisoner's board and lodging. However, unlike today, there were no lasting prison sentences designed to reform the unreformable. Prisoners lingered in gaol for only as long as it took to bring them to trial, and if pronounced guilty of a capital offence, committed to hang, or perhaps to transportation.

According to the *Mercury*, of the ten 'unfeeling monsters now secured in our County gaol' four were to be sentenced to hang, one to transportation, and five were freed.

Gang members John Smith Jnr, Thomas Malsbury, John Tack, Gilkes and possibly others, fled before they could be apprehended.

Chapter Seven
The Summer Assizes of 1787

Serious crimes, particularly those carrying a death sentence, were tried at the Court of Assizes. These were held twice a year before a professional High Court Judge and Grand Jury, which decided if there was a case to answer, and a Petty Jury that delivered the verdict. The Northampton Summer Assizes of 1787 were held at the Sessions House in George Row adjacent to the county gaol and house of correction. Eighteenth century trials provided excellent free entertainment and matters frequently got out of hand. Judges had trouble controlling the 'noisy, rude, curious, hardly restrainable low rabble forcing themselves into the court'. The *Mercury* reported the final charges brought against the men from the Culworth Gang:

John Smith the Elder, a labourer, age about fifty-three, and considered a very old offender, for robbing Mr Lemm of Foxley in the parish of Blakesley on the highway in the parish of Greens Norton, of a silver watch and fifteen shillings in money.

William Bowers, age about thirty-six, a labourer of Culworth, for breaking into the house of William Mayo and his wife of Sewell in the parish of Blakesley with others, between eleven and twelve o'clock on Thursday night 5th April, disguised in smocks and with handkerchiefs over their faces, armed with a pistol and bill hook, and stealing fifteen shillings in money, a gold ring, silver stock buckle, a coat and hat, several shirts, shifts and stockings, a woman's gown, a piece of new linen cloth, a flitch and a half of bacon, and several other articles.

Richard Law, age about thirty, a carpenter, born at Culworth, for robbing Edward Jackson on the highway near Towcester of a silver watch.

William Pettifer, alias Peckover, age about forty, a labourer, for robbing the son and servant of Mr Warren on the highway near Chipping Warden of four guineas and some silver.

The newspaper reported the four were convicted upon the clearest evidence.

Several other bills were preferred in case those upon which they were tried had not been sufficient to secure capital convictions, but these were not required. John Smith the Elder, William Bowers, Richard Law and William Pettifer were sentenced to death by hanging.

A petition was sent after the judge in favour of Law and Pettifer, presumably because they had made thirty confessions, but, 'his Lordship could not be prevailed to grant them any respite'. There was no other appeals procedure available before 1907.

John Smith the Elder was 'several times strongly importuned to disclose what he knew of the 1785 robbery of Mr Adams', mentioned in Chapter Six, for which James Tarry was wrongly hanged, as well as other robberies with which he had been concerned. He refused to make any confessions as was also the case with Bowers, 'and in this resolution they both persisted'. Indeed, Smith the Elder and William Bowers refused to make any discoveries right to the end. Bowers was described by the *Northampton Mercury* as 'the most hardened and abandoned that can be conceived, swearing and cursing upon every occasion'. When a witness testified, Bowers declared, loud enough to be heard in all parts of the court, that 'a man hath no more chance here than a cat in hell without claws.'

Although initially capitally convicted for his crimes, William Abbot the Sulgrave clerk had successfully petitioned the judge for a pardon, or at least a lesser sentence, in acknowledgement of the seventeen confessions he had made. In his case it worked and he was reprieved, and instead sentenced to transportation for life. Abbot was one of the first convicts to be the sent to Australia after General George Washington's success at the American War of Independence closed off America for convicts. King George III, less affectionately perhaps also known as Mad King George, is remembered for losing the American colonies. Gambia in West Africa was tried briefly but abandoned after quickly gaining the reputation of being a 'white man's grave'. English prisons were overcrowded with felons awaiting deportation and Sir Joseph Banks came up with the idea of sending them to Botany Bay. Sir Joseph was a botanist who had accompanied Captain Cook aboard HMS Endeavour on his trip to Australia.

Abbot missed the first convoy of eleven prison ships that departed Portsmouth bound for Australia on 13th May 1787. The prisons were so full he was detained during His Majesty's Pleasure on a renovated ship known as hulk, whilst awaiting transport on the next available convoy. No murderers or others convicted of a violent crime were sent to Australia. Convicts comprised many ordinary people forced to turn to crime in order to survive. When transportation to Australia became possible after 1787, the penalty for crimes such as cattle rustling was reduced from hanging to transportation. There was an ulterior motive of course, it was hoped the exiles would in time colonise the new world on behalf of England. However, initially, many convicts refused to work in the harsh conditions found in Australia. It is said Abbot was so weak when he arrived in Australia he had to crawl ashore.

William and Benjamin Smith, and Elizabeth and William Tyrell, and perhaps also Charles Dixon and John Lacy (who are otherwise unaccounted for), were delivered by proclamation. This means they were released without trial or verdict, perhaps through lack of evidence. In William Tyrells' case this is inexplicable, as he was implicated in multiple crimes by the confessions. Corruption and bribery were rife in the legal system during the eighteenth century, so there are any number of reasons why an accused person might be released. A favourite get-out for women was to 'plead their bellies' when they became pregnant in gaol. Gaolers sold access to prisoners to anyone willing to endure the stench and the risk of catching something.

It must have been a huge relief for those delivered by proclamation to be released from the stinking County gaol, which was often ravaged by lethal fevers.

The site of the executions at the White Elephant (former Kingsley Park Tavern) corner of Northampton Racecourse. When it was found that the previous site of the gallows came within an allotment, commissioners allocated one rood of land on the corner of the Racecourse for this purpose.

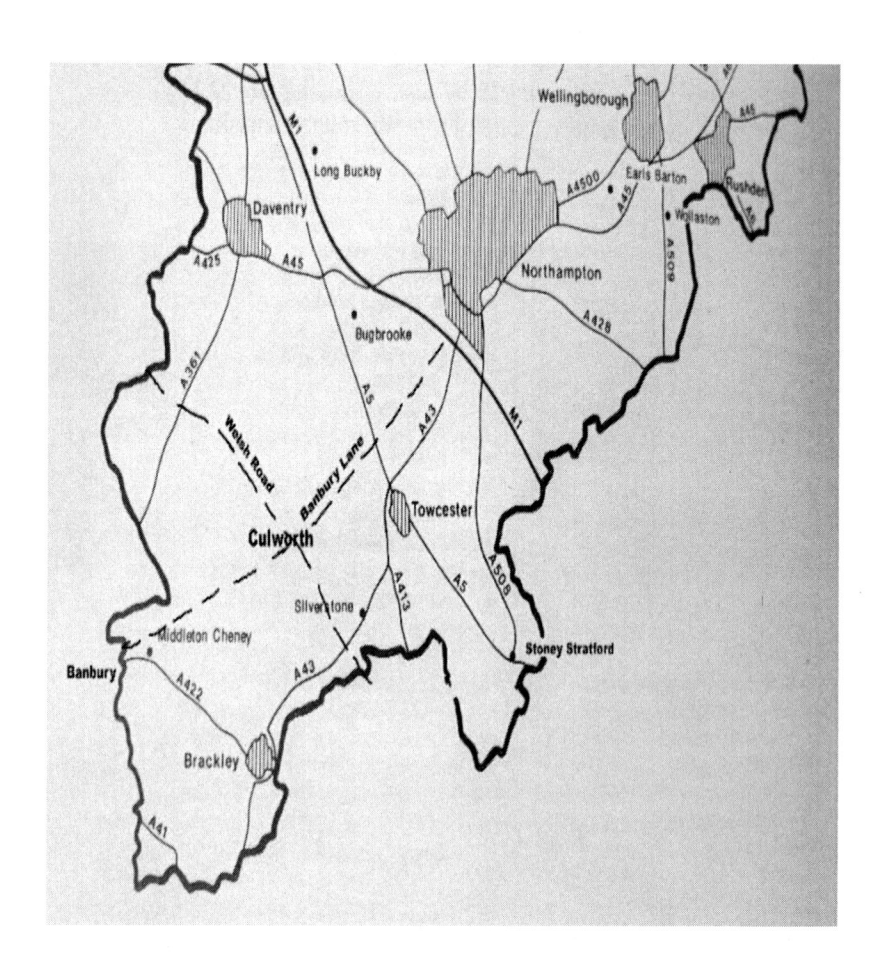

Map showing the approximate location of the village of Culworth in South Northamptonshire south west of the A5 Watling Street. Distances by turnpike (in miles) Banbury to Daventry 17, Brackley to Towcester 11, Towcester to Northampton 8, Daventry to Towcester 12. The dotted lines shown crossing at Culworth are the approximate position of the ancient drover's routes, the Banbury Lane and the Welsh Road. Map prepared by the author.

The early eighteenth-century barn at Fernhill Farm was converted into a house around 2009. The large barn atop Thorpe hills commands fine views in all directions and would have been an ideal lookout position for the Culworth Gang.

The initials WS, perhaps carved by William Smith whilst on lookout, seen high up on the stone reveal to the front entrance of Fernhill barn. Photographs of Fernhill barn taken by the author by kind permission of the owners Mr and Mrs Lombard.

Tom and Sid Cooknell outside Hangland Farm, around 1910. The isolated Farmhouse was built around 1775 after the enclosure of Wardington. It was traditionally constructed with stone and thatch, with two rooms on the ground floor, three bedrooms on the first floor and a large attic room on the second floor. A dairy extended the length of the house on the north side. Photo provided by current owners Mr and Mrs Ayres.

The only entrance into Hangland Farmhouse was secured by a sturdy oak beam which drew across the door to 'keep the Culworth Gang out'.

A ROBBERY!

WHEREAS the TURNPIKE-HOUSE at Hopper's-Ford, on the Turnpike-Road leading from Towcester to Brackley, in the County of Northampton, was feloniously entered by three Persons, all with their Faces black'd, and two with Carters Frocks, on Monday Evening the 17th of this instant March, 1783; who, after taking a few Shillings which were in the Pocket of Mrs. Blackwell, the Renter of the Tolls, stole from the House the following Articles, viz. Four Pair of Sheets; one Sheet marked with blue, No. 17; two Table-Cloths; some Napkins; three Lad's Shirts (one Holland and two Flaxen); three Men's Flaxen Shirts; five Pair of Sleeves, two Pair ruffled; one Pair of Jacket Sleeves, ruffled; one long Lawn Handkerchief; five double white Handkerchiefs; two black Silk Handkerchiefs; two red, white, and yellow Silk Handkerchiefs; one clear Lawn Apron; a fine Cambrick Apron, mark'd E D; one Holland Apron, mark'd E; four check'd Aprons, three with Bibs; two Pair of Gloves, one black Lamb, open Work within Side the Arm, the other white Kid; one black Silk Cloak, the Head lined with white Silk, trimmed with Love; a Silver Tea-Spoon; a Woollen Apron; nine double plain Caps; two laced Caps; three coloured Handkerchiefs; six Pillow Drawers; a Pair of Stays, Tabby Half Way, the other white Russel, round Tip, fine large Twist, very clean; two Pair brown knit ribb'd Stockings; three Yards of new Ribbon, and some Yards more; three Cheeses and a Half, and some Bread.

By Order of the Trustees of the said Turnpike-Road, this is to give Notice, that any Person or Persons who will discover the Offenders, or either of them, so as he or they may be convicted thereof, shall be entitled to a Reward of TEN GUINEAS, to be paid on such Conviction.

R. WESTON, Clerk to the said Trustees.

Aynho, 18th March, 1783.

The Northampton Mercury published this announcement offering a reward for information leading to the convictions of those responsible for the Hopper's-Ford robbery.

To the PUBLIC.

DIVINE Providence having lately, in Tenderneſs to a much-injured Public, led Juſtice by the Hand to the dark Retreats of the moſt numerous Set of abandoned Ruffians that perhaps have ever continued ſo long a Diſgrace to civil Government, or have been ſo ſucceſsfully combined in their Depredations on the peaceful and induſtrious Part of the Community; having for better than eighteen Years back, with the Inſtruments of Death in their Hands, daringly infeſted and robbed on the Highways, and ſpread Midnight Terrors through this and the neighbouring Counties; ſporting with the Fears and Spoils of their peaceful but defenceleſs Fellow-Creatures:---It is therefore hoped, as ten of thoſe unfeeling Monſters are now ſecured in our County Gaol, to take their Trials at the next Aſſizes to be holden for this County, that all Perſons, whether injured or not, who may have it in their Power to furniſh Evidence of their Guilt, will, on this Occaſion, ſhew a becoming Forwardneſs in their Endeavours to prevent theſe avowed Enemies of our ſocial Happineſs from being again turned looſe on the Public. In Order to which, the Attention of thoſe who are more particularly concerned, is earneſtly requeſted to the following Liſt of Goods not yet owned, but ſuſpected to be ſtolen, and to be ſeen at Maidford, in this County; as the owning of which in Time, may contribute, not only to bring Conviction Home to thoſe Delinquents already in Hold, but may alſo lead to a further Diſcovery of other their criminal Accomplices.

Maidford, June 19th, 1787. M. O. CLARE.

Liſt of ſtolen Goods, or Goods ſuſpected to be ſtolen:

One Silver Watch, made by Wm. Shan, London, No. 3182.
— N. B. The firſt Figure of this Watch is almoſt defaced.
Ditto Silver Watch, made by John Lamprey, Banbury, No. 2537.
Ditto, made by Wm. Tyrill, No. 2925.
Ditto, made by J. Williamſon, London, Number defaced.
Ditto, made by N. Plimer, Wellington, No. 134.
Ditto, made by J. Watſon, London. No Number.
— N. B. This laſt-mentioned Watch, with 20s. in Silver, was taken from the Perſons of two Men on Horſeback, returning from Biceſter Market, in the County of Oxford, about Michaelmas laſt, 1786; who are requeſted to come and own the ſame.

One plain Gold Ring, without Name or Mark, but the Stamp.
One Silver Half-Crown Piece (King William) with a particular Mark on the Croſs Side.
Ten Pair of Home-ſpun Sheets of a ſmall Size, ſome marked L. ſome M. H. with Pillow Evars and Towels.
Four home ſpun Shirts, two Holland Shirts marked T.
Several Silk Handkerchiefs, and ſome Cotton. Some fine Women's Cotton Stockings. Seven great Evats. Three black Silk Cloaks, two trimmed with black Lace. Several Women's Gowns and Petticoats. One Chintz Pattern Cotton Gown; two of fine Crape. A Mourning Silk Apron and Cloak; with ſeveral other Articles of Women's and Children's Apparel. Several Men's Hats, particularly one a French glaz'd Hat. Various Articles of Clock Wheels and Movements: With a conſiderable Number of Picklock Keys, particularly one a large bright Door Key. Some Cat Gut; new ſtriped Cotton Handkerchiefs, and Cotton in Pieces; ſome new Worſted Stockings, two Rolls of Flaxen Tape---all new, and ſeemingly the Plunder of ſome Shop.

Announcement published in the Northampton Mercury by Justice Rev O'Clare on Saturday 23rd June 1787.

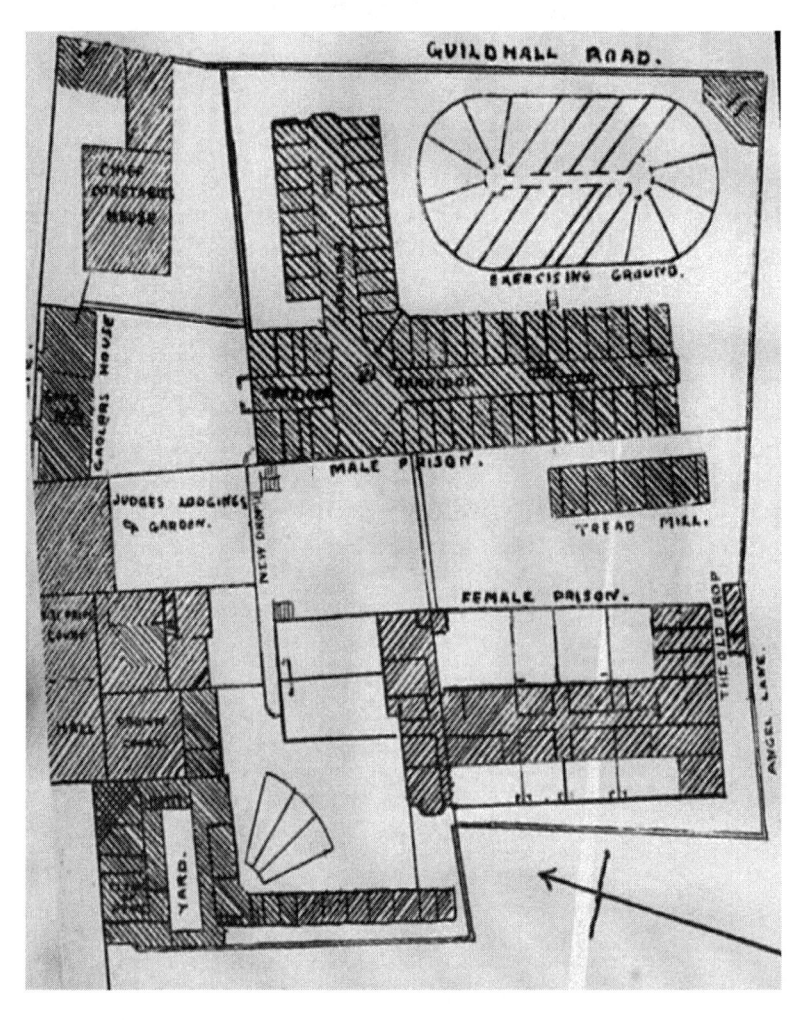

Northampton County gaol around 1800. Note the male prison and the female prison, the old drop where hangings could be witnessed by the public from Cow Meadow, and the more discrete new drop, used for multiple hangings. Also, note the dreaded punishment tread mill. The new drop design was first used at Newgate prison in 1783 after boisterous crowds attending hangings became completely out of hand.

Northampton Sessions House.

Valerie and Michelle Pettifer's copies of letters written by the gang. Originals at Banbury Museum.

> 1787
>
> Given to Mr William
> Page Farmer of
> Culworth
> 1787
>
> Pray all young men a warning take
> By the Culworth gang and their fate
> Found guilty all of robbery
> Now are to hang on the gallows tree
>
> Farewell all friends and relations dear
> No more in Culworth shall we appear
>
> Take our advice bad company for to shun
> Shun not this warning before it is too late
>
> God Bye my aged parents, my
> wife and children dear
> No more to meet upon this earth
> our time is drawing near
> when us are dead and in our graves
> Pray think of the warning that
> to you we gave

Letter given to Mr William Page Farmer of Culworth, 1787.

Chapter Eight
The Gang's Final Letters

Whilst awaiting execution the four condemned men spent their time reading and praying. William Pettifer is reported to have undergone conversion to religion whilst in the gaol, although this may have been a ruse as we read in chapter four, he had twice been married in Culworth church, and he had been christened in Paulerspury in 1747. The gaol chapel was in the upper room of the house of Mr Scofield, the gaoler. It was painful for prisoners loaded with irons to go up and down the stairs, especially for those held in the dungeon which was eleven steps underground.

The men composed a letter to Mr William Page, a Culworth farmer, from prison. Although many poor people were illiterate, some had been taught to read and write after the English Civil War. Although farmer Page had been victim of the gang's attention himself in the past, losing some geese, a poem supposedly written by Smith Snr at the time had apologised:

Dear Mr Page
Don't get in a rage
We bought your geese
For a penny apiece
And left the money
with the gander.

It is not recorded why the gang should write to Mr Page. Perhaps he was the only person they could think of in the village who could read. It is thought Mr Page's two sons, James and Richard, may have been slightly involved with the gang, and presumably Page had forgiven John Smith by then for stealing his geese.

***

Valerie and Michelle Pettifer of Cogenhoe kindly supplied copies of letters written by the gang for inclusion in this book. It is believed the originals are held at Banbury Museum. Their distant relation,

William Pettifer, signed the letter to Mr Page on behalf of the four condemned gang members. As might be expected, various spellings of names appear from time to time in newspaper reports and articles etc. He signed himself J Petifer rather than W Pettifer. Nicknames and alias were frequently used so that real names couldn't easily be extracted under duress by the authorities. Valerie's research in the 1980s found the name Peckover was formerly spelt Pickenhaver, sometimes corrupted to Pettifer. The unedited letter reads:

1787 The Culworth Gang of Petifer Bowers Law, J Tyrell and 3 Smiths of Culworth

Dear Mr Page
This is to inform you that we have all made our last dying speech and confession they have found us all guilty and us are the sentenced to be hanged for housebreaking and robbery.
Dear Mr William Page if us could right what us have done wrong but it is to late now us is in jail lay in a dreary cell condemned to die if us had took the advice of our aged parents Dear Mr Page please to give our kindest love to all our relations and friends that are at Culworth and us send our kindest love to you and your two sons James and Richard and all your family and may the Lord have mercy upon us
Dear Mr Page I hope you will tell all young men that you meet with to take warning by our sad fate this is our advice to all young men bad company forsake and read and study the Bible.
So farewell Mr William Page
J Petifer
Please to give this to Mr William Page farmer of Culworth

Pray all young men a warning take
By the Culworth gang and their sad fate
Found guilty all of robbery.
Now to hang on the gallows tree
Farewell all friends and relations dear
No more in Culworth shall we appear

Take our advice bad company forsake
Shun not this warning before it is too late
Good Bye my aged parents my
Wife and children dear
No more to meet upon this earth
Our time is drawing near
When us are dead and in our graves
Pray think of this warning that to you us gave.

John Smith the Elder also left a beautiful letter to his wife, dated 21 July, 1787 expressing his feelings on his approaching death. The unedited letter reads:

My dear and loving Wife,
THESE come with my kind Love to you and all my dear Children, begging you will come to see me before I depart this wicked World, and beg of God to forgive me all my Sins, and I will endeavour to make my Peace with God before I die. My dear I desire my Son William will make my Coffin, and let me have it here before I die; and I desire you will have my Body taken Home to my own House, that you may see me buried: And beg of my Children to take warning by my unhappy State, that they may turn to the Paths of Virtue; and beg of them to beware of bad Company and Sabbath breaking, which is the Prayer of a dying Father. My Dear, I hope you will come to see me, and let my Daughter Molly know, that she may meet you here, for I cannot die in Peace without I do see her, so I beg you will desire her to come,
So no more, from you dying Husband,
JOHN SMITH
PS:
My dear, desire my son John to marry Elizabeth Beard, and beg of him to be good to her and the child, and take warning by me that they may live in comfort. I desire you will take care of these lines and cause them to be read to all my children every Sabbath Day, and I hope that God will give them grace to take warning – it is the prayer of a dying father.

Unfortunately, John Smith Jnr didn't heed his father's advice and was executed along with William Tyrell for another highway robbery in 1788 (see Chapter Ten).

William Pettifer wrote a final letter written shortly before his execution admitting to his crimes. He confessed that the gang had robbed scores of houses, which 'us all do repent'.

The prison chaplain, or ordinary, would often publish the confessions and final words of any notable prisoners to sell at the hangings, even if he had to make them up himself for pamphlets to be printed in time! Rising literacy in the late eighteenth century ensured great demand for salacious stories and there were many lurid publications available to titillate the reader. Stories about crime were equally popular, for they addressed many of the insecurities felt at the time.

Chapter Nine
The Hangings

Having received the sacrament and taken their last farewell to their friends the felons were put into two carts. The mournful procession moved off from Northampton County gaol a little after ten o'clock on Friday morning 3rd August 1787. They were accompanied by the chaplain and their gaolers, and greeted enthusiastically by many well-wishers along the way.

John Smith the Elder, Richard Law and William Pettifer, alias Peckover, all convicted of highway robbery, went in the first cart. William Bowers, convicted for housebreaking, together with two, unconnected, robbers from Desborough went in the second cart. These two Desborough men, David Coe and John Hulbert, were both aged about thirty, and their occupation was weavers. They were condemned to death for the night time robbery of a flitch [side] of bacon and a quantity of pork worth thirty shillings from the house of John Loake of Desborough, a victualler.

The procession paused at the outskirts of the town for a drink at the Bantam Cock public house. This practice of a final drink provided very good business for publicans, particularly when there was a large crowd gathering for the anticipated entertainment of rousing final speeches. The right of the condemned to speak before their execution was celebrated in English society. Convention dictated that convicts should make a full confession and repentance of their sins in a speech from the gallows, to enable the condemned to face God with a clear conscience.

The population of Northampton was around 7,000 at the time, and the vast majority appear to have made the most of the occasion. About 5,000 attended according to the newspaper, the town's folk treating it as a public holiday. There hadn't been a hanging in Northampton since March, and now there were half a dozen at once. The *Mercury* reported *'the concourse of persons who attended the execution was very great'*. Many highwaymen were proud of their profession and were generally wished well by the crowds on their way to the gallows.

It wasn't however a record turnout for a Northampton Racecourse hanging. An estimated twelve to fifteen thousand spectators attended in August 1735 when twenty-year-old Elizabeth Fawson of Weston and Weedon on Banbury Lane was hung for poisoning her husband after six weeks of marriage.

The cortege proceeded across open countryside to the former quarry at the Poor Fields on Northampton Heath. The men, no doubt by now a little unsteady after a good drink, were probably sitting on coffins in the carts.

The scaffold might have been a triangular wooden structure, usually erected the night before the hangings. Gallows could be put up and taken down like goalposts. Fortunately, the site of the hangings was far enough away from the gaol so that the hammering would not have disturbed the condemned men's beauty sleep, although it might have awoken those residing nearby at the Kingsley Park Tavern (now renamed the White Elephant as horse racing was abandoned at the park after 1904 following a number of serious accidents).

A rope placed around each man's neck was fixed to the cross beam as they stood, three to a cart. At noon, on a given signal, perhaps a person dropping a hat, the cart was pulled swiftly forward leaving the men dangling a short distance off the ground. The newspaper reported the conduct of the condemned; 'their behaviour was very suitable to persons in their unhappy situation, they all acknowledged the justice of their sentence and begged the surrounding multitude to take warning by their untimely end. Around noon, after time spent in prayer, they were launched into eternity.'

Sometimes, victims of hangings appeared to die instantly; others were not so fortunate. If onlookers considered the condemned were taking too long to die, they might pull down on their legs until struggling ceased. Hence the expression, 'pulling your leg'.

There was an ancient custom that women rushed forward to place the hand of a dead man upon their own bodies, supposedly to cure warts. There had been a few scares in the past when the act of placing a hand on a woman's warm breast had caused the man to come around!

After hanging for half an hour, the time required by law, the bodies were taken down. There was considerable debate in the country at the time as to whether those executed by hanging died of strangulation or spinal dislocation. After 1752 a surgeon was required to dissect the necks of the executed and, if finding the spinal column intact, declare the cause of death to be strangulation. The idea that after death their body would be cut up was terrifying, it added an additional punishment to the hanging.

The bodies would be stripped and delivered to friends for interment. The usual practice was for the gaolers to take the victim's clothes, which were highly prized as souvenirs, and would no doubt sell for a good price on Northampton Market.

Three of the gang members' bodies were returned to Culworth for burial. Written in brackets after the three names in the parish records are the words 'Hanged at Northampton for Highway Robbery'. Friends and relatives probably guarded the graves for a couple of weeks as a precaution against body snatchers, for the theft of cadavers for medical research was a common occurrence.

William Bower's body was not claimed, and the hangman's assistant arranged disposal at a 'convenient place', possibly St Giles' churchyard which had been used before for this purpose. All baptised people were entitled to a burial with religious ceremony, whether they attended church regularly or not, unless excommunicate, or the cause of death was suicide. Perhaps his girlfriend Elizabeth Tyrell, the mother of his two-year-old child, who was also called William Bowers, was still in custody.

In time it was considered the march of the condemned through public streets was not in accordance with the growing sentiment of the people. In 1818 executions in Northampton were moved to the County gaol, where crowds could be better controlled whilst watching the hangings from Angel Lane and Cow Meadow. The Capital Punishment (Amendment) Act 1868 finally ended public executions in the United Kingdom.

Chapter Ten
The Aftermath of the Hangings

Less than a year later, on 1st April 1788, William Tyrell, who had been one of the fortunate gang members delivered by proclamation from the 1787 Northampton Summer Assizes, was executed at Warwick. Quite why he was released from Northampton gaol was inexplicable to many, as he had been clearly implicated by Law and Pettifer in over twenty of the Culworth Gang's robberies.

Tyrell, aged around thirty-eight, was finally condemned to death for robbing John Bricknell on the highway near the Gaydon Inn (in Warwickshire) on 23rd February 1788. He stole five shillings, a canvas purse, a pocket knife and sundry papers. Tyrell, described in the newspaper as an 'old offender . . . during the whole of his confinement behaved in a most audacious and hardened manner. He refused in prison to join in prayer with the clergyman and his fellow sufferers. On his way to the place of execution he seemed totally unaffected with his deplorable situation and even only five minutes before he was launched into eternity, laughed at the executioner, who offered him an orange. He denied the robbery but acknowledged he had been guilty of many others, and had always shared in the spoils of the Culworth Gang.'

John Smith the Elder had entreated his son John Jnr to forgo crime and to marry the mother of his child, Elizabeth Beere (incorrectly spelt Beard in the gang's final letter) from Claydon, the young daughter of the village blacksmith. Nevertheless, in May 1788, he was apprehended in Oxfordshire and committed to Warwick Gaol charged with being concerned together with William Tyrell in the robbery of Mr Bricknell.

John Smith Jnr was capitally convicted and condemned to death. When there was some confusion as to Smith's true identity during the trial, he interrupted the judge mid flow and told him to be careful as he had sentenced the wrong man to death in the case of James Tarry (see Chapter Six). Before his execution, Smith made a full confession of the robbery for which Tarry had been hanged. In the church register entry for Tarry's burial is a sad handwritten note: 'He was innocent of the crime for which he suffered.'

Elizabeth Beere attended her lover's hanging and had the body delivered to her. With a donkey and a pair of panniers she conveyed it back to Culworth for interment. Elizabeth trudged the twenty miles from Warwick to Culworth through the night, a feat described as *'Thus exhibiting an instance of constancy of devotion rarely exceeded.'* Elizabeth, too, was dead within a year, apparently leaving behind five children.

***

John and Elizabeth Smith's elder son William did, however, become a reformed character. He remained in Culworth and eventually worked as a domestic servant for the same family for twenty years. There is still a strong belief around the local parishes that other members of the gang were rounded up at Fernhill barn on the high ground between Thorpe Mandeville and Upper Wardington and summarily executed somewhere in the vicinity. It has been suggested that the names of nearby Hangland Farm and Hanginghill Barn corroborate the story. The author isn't convinced, and agrees with Frank and Linda Ayres, the current owners of Hangland Farm, that it is more likely the farm names derive from the nature of the steep western slope of the land where field names include Big Hangland and Little Hangland.

Dave Hewitt of Bugbrooke History Society believes there was an ancient 'hanging tree' on Banbury Lane, but doesn't know whether it is still there. The story was that a robber hung for stealing the mail had been left hanging in a metal cage to rot, as a deterrent to others. When a passer-by noticed the condemned man was not quite dead, he shot him!

Chapter Eleven
Close to the Wind

Cropredy near Culworth, where the Civil War battle took place in 1644, is perhaps better known nowadays for its music festival. It was established by folk and rock band Fairport Convention in the mid-1970s. The group recorded a ballad written by former Guilsborough school head teacher Stuart Marson called 'Close to the Wind' a pleasant, although somewhat chilling, song, with the lyrics: 'fifteen children of Culworth, well, their fathers are taken away'. If true about the number of orphans, it is hardly surprising there are still descendants and relatives of gang members living locally. If John Smith the Elder had at least four children, William Pettifer Six, John Smith Jnr five, William Bowers and William Tyrell at least one apiece, it is not unrealistic to agree there were at least fifteen children who lost their fathers to the hangman.

The lyrics to the ballad are shown below, by kind permission of Stuart. He wrote the song around 1979/80 after reading an article about the Culworth Gang in the local Northampton paper the *Chronicle and Echo*. The words are taken from Stuart Marson's own version recorded on his album Where Falcons Fly. The name 'Nancy' in the first verse is purely Stuart's invention. Although, perhaps by coincidence, Richard Ferguson, aka Galloping Dick, a well-known highwayman from the 1780s, had a girlfriend called Nancy.

Close to the Wind
Farewell to you, my faithful Nancy
And a thousand times adieu;
For the constable comes up from Brackley Market
And a hundred volunteers too.
No more can we hide in the forest
I fear they would run us to ground
And the wild sea, we sailed upon it
Too close to the wind.

For twenty long years, we have roamed the highways
Of Northamptonshire.
From Daventry down to the southern byways
Oh, we've robbed both the rich and the poor.
For oft times our families were starving
With the highway that kept them alive,
And the wild sea, we sailed upon it
Too close to the wind.

And tonight, I lie in a darkened dungeon
Condemned on the gallows to die,
While the man who sent us away is only
Bound for Australia.
No man will stand to defend us
Well, there's nought but abuse comes our way,
And the wild sea, we sailed upon it
Too close to the wind.

And the clouds they rise on Northampton market,
And the crowds pour into the town,
And people will crowd in these streets till sunset,
When the hangman cuts us down.
And fifteen children of Culworth
Well, their fathers are taken away,
And the wild sea we sailed upon it
Too close to the wind

Chapter Twelve
Final Thoughts

A little is known of the fate of some of the other gang members. Thomas Malsbury returned to Culworth, where he was run over a few years later by a horse and cart and killed. Quite how he avoided prosecution after being named in four of the confessions is another interesting question. Perhaps it was a case of who you know rather than what you know for, as previously mentioned in chapter seven, bribery was commonplace amongst officials at the time. Similarly, with William Abbot. He admitted taking part in thirteen robberies and was spared hanging despite initially being capitally convicted. Pettifer's name appeared in the confessions thirteen times, and Law's fourteen, and both were hung, even though they provided thirty of the confessions in mitigation.

John Tack, another of those who avoided arrest, was never heard from again. It appears he hadn't provided very well for his family for it is written that his 'old father was entirely maintained by the parish, even to the extent of a payment for delousing'.

Mr Gilkes (pronounced Jilkes) was said to have joined the gang 'for the excitement and romance which attended their excursions'. Perhaps he was similar in appearance to his relative John Gilkes of Moreton Pinkney, described by Rev Mozley as 'good looking, and well-mannered and educated, sporting a fine beard, and was finely dressed in a green velveteen suit. The most ornamental figure in the village, evidently a gamekeeper in office, and a poacher out of it'. John Gilkes was reputedly also closely linked to the gang but was never actually convicted of anything.

Highwayman Gilkes was one of those who disappeared at the time of the arrests in 1787. He fled to the Indies where he made a fortune from the plantations, and possibly the slave trade. In later life he returned to England but died shortly afterwards from an illness contracted on the journey. His relatives reputedly found very little money on him and no papers whatsoever. His fortune was never found.

The above story is corroborated by Dave Hewitt who is related to the Gilkes family by marriage. He told the author it was a very large family, with many members based in North Oxfordshire, some with biblical names such as Elizer, Moses and Job. Another of the Gilkes family, Thomas, was a sawyer and also a barber. The family still have one of the great two-man cross cut saws used to fell trees for pit props in the days before steam saws and chainsaws. Uncle Tom, as Dave Hewitt describes him, became butler to the landowning Thorntons of Brockhall, mentioned in chapter four. Tom Gilkes was notably light fingered and was dismissed after being snared in a sting involving marked coins in the collection plate.

Dave Hewitt has seen a list of names of those who benefitted from the £20m compensation paid out under the Slavery Abolition Act of 1833. The name Gilkes appears a number of times, but of course we shouldn't condemn or judge what happened in history by modern standards. The wealthy Bond family of Culworth also had links with the slave trade through plantations in the Indies. They retained a former slave as their butler. Charles Bacchus was buried in Culworth churchyard in 1762 and has an impressive memorial headstone near the church porch.

Whether anyone connected with the gang benefited in the long run from their criminal activities is unknown, although perhaps unlikely. William Pettifer's widow and John Tack's father were entirely maintained by parish relief, for there was no welfare state to look after the poor until the following century. Gang members Thomas Malsbury, William Pettifer and John Tack are also recorded as having been recipients of payments under the Poor Law system. Part of the funding was derived from the income received from thirty-four acres of charity land in the parish. Jack Gould's article in Northamptonshire Past and Present 2000 says that after 1790 William Smith appears in the accounts of the Overseers of the Poor because he became a roundsman, the name given to unemployed men in the parish who were required to go from farm to farm until they found a job as casual labourers, when their wages were paid half by the farmer and half from the parish. Presumably it was after this time that he became a trusted servant for twenty years.

The men responsible for bringing the Culworth Gang's criminal activities to an end perhaps fared a lot better. Presumably they collected some hefty reward money from the courts, the government and the victims of some of the numerous crimes. Courts awarded generous sums to thief takers and others solving crimes and recovering stolen goods. The government typically paid up to £100, over £15,000 in today's terms, for convictions leading to execution. At a time when a typical wage was around £7 per annum these were very large sums indeed. George Barker's History and Antiquities of the county of Northampton 1841 records that the Rev Michael O'Clare received 'the thanks of the grand jury of the county for his able and indefatigable exertions as a magistrate in discovering and bringing to justice the notorious Culworth gang of housebreakers and highwaymen, who were the terror of this and the neighbouring counties for nearly twenty years'. O'Clare's enmity against the Culworth Gang appears to have paid off. Maidford village records show he secured a great deal of land for himself at the time of the enclosures.

***

Were the Culworth Gang unique in England at the time? Perhaps not, as Dave Hewitt has been told more than once during his talks about similar gangs operating in other parts of the country. Rural life was very insular in those days. For hundreds of years droving had been a major part of rural life, not only through the herding of livestock to markets but also the carrying of news from faraway places. News travelled very slowly, at the pace of the herds.

Until recent years there has been a noticeable reluctance to talk about the gang amongst some secretive villagers, who perhaps knew more than they were willing to divulge. Dave Hewitt remembers being told one had to be very careful what one said to any member of certain families in South Northamptonshire villages in the old days, some of whom were possibly of gipsy descent and exceptionally protective of one another. Rev Moseley wrote of one gipsy lady relocating from a camp to a cottage to give birth, and by the time she had reached the age of eighty she was the matriarchal head of a hundred villagers!

The 1965 edition of the Banbury History Society magazine Cake and Cockhorse includes James Beesley's account of the activities of the gang first published in 1837/8. His account drew freely on the memory of those who remembered the incidents described. The 1965 magazine confirmed that a considerable amount of research had been done on the Culworth Gang since 1838, though regrettably very little has been published.

Hopefully this book will help keep their story alive. Certainly, it should finally convince a certain good friend of the author's that the Culworth Gang were named after a village and not an individual!

The End

Appendix

Culworth Gang members arrested and charged with offences in April 1787

1. John Smith the Elder, labourer 1734-1787 m Elizabeth Tack in 1761
2. William Smith, b1762, labourer, later a servant
3. Benjamin Smith
4. William Bowers, labourer b. circa 1751-1787
5. Richard Law, carpenter b. circa 1757-1787
6. William Pettifer alias Peckover, labourer 1747-1787 m (1) Mary White 1766, m (2) Martha Justin 1768
7. William Abbot, shoemaker. Clerk of Sulgrave Parish
8. William Tyrell/Tervill/Terrill/Turrell or Turrill) labourer 1750-1788 m Martha Gibbs of Culworth in 1775 (executed at Warwick)
9. Charles Dixon
10. John Lacy of Sulgrave (friend of William Abbot)
11. Elizabeth Tyrell (William Bower's girlfriend)

Culworth Gang members sentenced to death by hanging at Northampton Summer Assizes 1787

1. John Smith the Elder
2. Richard Law
3. William Pettifer alias Peckover
4. William Bowers
5. William Abbot

Sentence commuted to transportation to Australia

1. William Abbot

Delivered by Proclamation (Released)

1. William Smith
2. Benjamin Smith
3. William Tyrell (hung at Warwick for highway robbery in 1788)

4. Elizabeth Tyrell, William Bowers' girlfriend

Fate not known
1. Charles Dixon
2. John Lacy

Absconded before arrest
1. John Smith Jnr. 1763-1788. (Hung at Warwick with William Tyrell.)
2. Thomas Malsbury, labourer, died in cart accident in Culworth
3. John Tack possibly related to Elizabeth Smith wife of John Smith the Elder
4. The mysterious Mr Gilkes who fled to the Indies

Named in the 1777 Northamptonshire Militia List
1. William Smith
2. Richard Law
3. William Tyrell
4. William Abbot/Abbott

Other possible gang members - names found in various sources during research
1. William Abbott, labourer from Sulgrave, possible relative of William Abbot the shoemaker?
2. Richard Jack, labourer of Culworth, mentioned in Beesley's 1841 account as being a prominent member of the gang. Possibly the same man as John Tack who absconded? -see above
3. Mr Cooknell, according to his distant relative Annette Taylor née Cooknell (see below), who lived at Fernhill Farm where gang members reputedly hid following the arrests in 1787.
4. Mr Watts of Wardington. A former village postman, another Mr Watts, alleged he was related to a gang member and also thought there had been two or three gang members from Wardington.
5. John Gilkes of Moreton Pinkney

6 and 7. Richard and John Page, sons of the Mr William Page the gang wrote to from gaol.

Several other unknown gang members had died before the arrests in 1787.

Acknowledgements

Research for this book benefited from considerable assistance from numerous sources, particularly the following. Apologies to any left out - names in alphabetical order.

- Ayres, Linda and Frank, of Hangland Farm Wardington who provided fascinating information on the history of their farm and surrounding areas.
- Benady (née Bowers) Ann, of Rose Hill Farm Grendon, the author's second cousin, for her knowledge (little though she admits it is) of her distant relative William Bowers of the Culworth Gang. Ann's father's full name was Thornton Richard Bowers 1895-1978, through the Brockhall connection, and he was always known as Thorn.
- Boasman, Rebecca, administrator of Culworth C of E Primary Academy for making enquiries and suggesting leads for research
- Breakspear, John, of Bazeley Farm Upper Wardington for sharing his knowledge of the gang.
- Cherry, Roger, of Dial House Farm Sulgrave whose family lived at Fernhill Farm in the eighteenth century, for passing on his recollections.
- Collins, Anne, of Northamptonshire Central Library for providing the invaluable copy of a broadsheet with the Culworth Gang's final speeches and list of confessions.
- Constant, Simon, of Wardington for showing great interest in the project from the start and for providing names and addresses of local people willing to be interviewed. Simon intriguingly pointed out there is a house called Pettifers close by the Peckover's Home Farm in Wardington.
- Crouch, Peter, detectorist of Towcester for providing encouragement for the project and giving the author a stage coach token from 1787 found at Grendon.

- Hewitt, Dave, of Bugbrooke History Group and speaker on the Culworth Gang. For several informative chats with the author and providing a wealth of information from his years of research, much of which is included in this book.
- Lombard, Ann and William, of Fernhill Farm Thorpe Mandeville, for allowing the author to inspect the carvings inside Fernhill barn, and providing information relating to the gang.
- Marson, Stuart, composer of the ballad 'Close to the Wind' recorded by Fairport Convention. The fact that Fairport Convention thought the story of the Culworth Gang worth recording impressed upon the author it was a subject well worth investigating. Stuart has also recorded the song on his own CD *Where Falcons Fly*. The author frequently enjoyed listening to Stuart's calming voice singing his emotionally evocative ballads whilst writing. Copies of Stuart's music are available directly on request; stuartmarson@sky.com
- O'Neill, Helen, (dec'd) formerly of Yardley Hastings, the author's first cousin who left written notes relating to their shared maternal grandmother Olive Blacklee (née Bowers') and the possible family connection to William Bowers of the Culworth Gang. Olive Bowers' father's full name was Richard Thornton Bowers 1859-1936. He was born at Dodford, south of Watling Street.
- Pettifer, Valerie and Michelle, distant relatives of gang member William Pettifer, for freely providing their own research material including the copies of the Gang's final letters.
- Rowling, Martin, clerk to Culworth parish and former village blacksmith, for providing a number of leads for research. Mr Rowling was able to confirm that Ralph Taylor, described as the *unofficial Culworth historian* in an article in the Chronicle and Echo from August 1979, died in 1984 aged ninety-one. The newspaper report said Mr Taylor's family 'came to neighbouring Sulgrave in 1636. He possessed a notebook full of details of the gang, some of the notes copied down from his father's memory.'

Unfortunately, the whereabouts of the notebook today are unknown and a possible wealth of information about the gang is awaiting rediscovery.
- Taylor (née Cooknell), Annette, related to a gang member called Cooknell and whose family were tenant fruit farmers at Hangland Farm Wardington, purchasing as sitting tenants in 1909.
- Vaughan, Robert, researcher for Cogenhoe and Whiston Heritage Society, who as always has proved a fund of knowledge about the old days in Northamptonshire, and freely shared his knowledge about the gang in the form of period newspaper cuttings, etc.
- Weller, Angela, Clerk to the PCC of Byfield who has assisted with local knowledge.
- Wiffill, Alexandra, Sec to the PCC of St Peter and St Paul Maidford for providing information about Rev Michael O'Clare.

Robberies committed by the Culworth Gang according to the confessions of Richard Law and William Pettifer, alias Peckover (nos 1-30) and William Abbot (nos 31-47)

The list is based on the Last Dying Speech and Confession broadsheet published by the *Northampton Mercury* provided by Northamptonshire Central Library.

1. Tyrell and Bowers robbed Mr. Groves of Sulgrave fifteen years ago.
2. Malsbury, Tyrell, and the servant-man of Mr. Pettum, robbed the house of Mr. Pettum, of Lawsfield, about fifteen years ago, of a hundred pounds.
3. Pettifer, John Smith the Elder and Tyrell, robbed the house of Mr. Ruth, between Silson [Silverstone] and Abthorpe, about nine years ago.

4. Thomas Malsbury and William Smith, in 1785, robbed Mr. Wright, attorney at law, of Field-Burcott of all his money and papers.
5. Law, Tyrell, and Bowers, robbed William Cotton the Banbury newsman, on Banbury Lane near Hunsbury Hill Northampton in November 1784.
6. Tyrell, Bowers and Law robbed Hopper's-Ford toll-gate-house near Whitfield on the Brackley to Towcester turnpike in 1783.
7. John Smith Jnr, Tyrell, and Law, robbed Mr. Rutledge of Hellidon.
8. Law and Tyrell robbed Edward Jackson of a silver watch on the highway coming from Towcester (For which Law suffered)
9. Tyrell, Bowers and Law, robbed Mr. Higham coming from Towcester fair.
10. Law, Pettifer, John Smith the Elder, John Smith Jnr, and William Smith robbed the Rev Mr. Wilkinson on a Sunday.
11. John Smith Jnr, Pettifer and Law robbed Mr. Warren's servant and son on the highway near Chipping Warden of four guineas and some silver (for which Pettifer suffered).
12. John Smith the Elder, John Smith Jnr, William Smith, Pettifer, Tyrell, Bowers, and Law, robbed Mr. Richardson, the Oxford Carrier near to Sturdy's Castle on the eighteenth of January, 1785.
13. Law, Pettifer, and Tyrell, stole the sheep of Mr. Jones's of Culworth.
14. John Smith the Elder, John Smith Jnr Law, and William Smith, robbed Cockley-House.
15. Malsbury, Tyrell, and Bowers robbed Mr. Maffey of Nethercutt in Warwickshire.
16. John Smith the Elder, William Smith, Tyrell, Bowers and Law robbed Hunt's Mill, near Westbury.
17. John Smith the Elder, William Smith, Tyrell, and Law robbed Mr. Freeman of Greatworth-Grounds.
18. John Smith the Elder, Tyrell and Pettifer robbed Mr. Wyatt of Sulgrave-Grounds, about nine years ago.

19. Law, Pettifer, John Smith the Elder and William Smith robbed Mr Stockley's house at Warden Hill.
20. John Smith the Elder, Bowers and Pettifer robbed Mr Dean's house at Culworth of some bacon. Bowers had Pettifer's share.
21. John Smith the Elder, Bowers, Pettifer and Tyrell robbed the house of Mr Gostelow of Adson Grounds.
22. Bowers and Tyrell robbed Mrs Linnell of Thorpe-Mandeville of bacon and meat.
23. John Smith the Elder, Bowers, Pettifer and Tyrell robbed Mrs Flowers of Chitwood House near Buckingham
24. John Smith the Elder, Tyrell and Pettifer robbed a stocking maker of his bags between Towcester and Abthorpe.
25. John Smith the Elder, John Smith Jnr, Tyrell and William Smith robbed Chalton Mill.
26. John Smith the Elder, Bowers and Tyrell robbed the house of Mr Toms of Farndon.
27. John Smith the Elder, John Smith Jnr, William Smith, Law, Pettifer and Tyrell robbed Mr Mitchell, brickmaker, at Cropredy House.
28. John Smith the Elder, John Smith Jnr, William Smith, Tyrell and Bowers attempted to rob the house of Mr Eaglestone in the parish of Wolverton, near Stony Stratford, on Sunday night, 23rd of November 1783.
29. John Smith the Elder, with his two sons, Bowers, and Tyrell robbed a turnpike house on their return from the attempted robbery in Wolverton.
30. John Smith the Elder, Pettifer and Tyrell robbed Elizabeth Thornton's house at Adson, Cropredy.
31. In April 1786, John Tack and William Abbot stole a lamb from a Ground by Foster's Booth.
32. William Bowers, Tack and Abbot robbed a man and woman near Hanslope of nine shillings and a coat.
33. John Smith the Elder, Tack and Abbot robbed two men coming from Stow on the Wold fair in October 1786, one of ten and six the other of fifteen shillings.

34. The same week the same men robbed two men near Bicester of a watch and about eighteen shillings.
35. On St Andrew's day, John Smith the Elder, John Smith Jnr, Tack and Abbot robbed two men between Brackley and Hinton, one of two and a half guineas, the other of about thirty shillings, a silver watch, a hat and handkerchief.
36. On St Thomas' day 1785, John Smith the Elder and William Abbot robbed a traveller on horseback of between four and five pounds, between Towcester and Plumb Park Corner.
37. About Christmas last, John Smith the Elder, and William Abbot robbed a man on foot near Chacombe of fourteen shillings, his hat, and shoes.
38. Last March, John Smith the Elder, William Smith and Abbot robbed Mr. Owen of his watch, nine and a half guineas and his hat, by Hopcroft's-Holt.
39. John Smith the Elder, William Smith, and Abbot, broke into a barn near Boddington and stole an axe and a handsaw.
40. The same men broke into another barn in that neighbourhood and stole a handsaw, a bag, a pair of hay-steelyards and a spade.
41. John Smith the Elder, Tack and Abbot killed a sheep near Helmdon.
42. John Smith the Elder and Abbot killed a sheep near Chacombe.
43. John Smith the Elder, John Smith Jnr, William Smith, Tack and Abbot broke into a house near Fenny-Compton and stole some shirts, sheets, and butter.
44. John Smith the Elder, Tack and Abbot stole a sheep near Wardington.
45. John Smith the Elder, John Smith Jnr, William Smith, Tack and Bowers robbed a tailor of some stays and stockings, by road.
46. John Lacy and Abbot robbed a fish-pond at Thorpe-Mandeville in 1785.
47. Thomas Malsbury and two of the Smiths robbed William Adams near Chipping Warden. A crime for which James Tarry was unjustly tried and convicted at the Summer Assizes 1785,

and executed at Northampton on Friday the 22nd of July the same year.

Bibliography

Baker, G. 1841. History and Antiquities of the county of Northampton. London: John Bowyer Nichols and son Parliament Street and John Rodwell, New Bond Street

Beesley, A. 1841. The History of Banbury. London: Nichols and Son

Beesley J. 1965 Cake and Cockhorse. Banbury: Banbury Historical Society. The article was first published in the first three numbers of the Manuscript Magazine of the Banbury Mechanics' Institute in December 1837, January 1838 and February 1838

Blacklee, R. 2018. Highwaymen Hangings and Heroes. Corby: 3P Publishing

Brandon, D 2001 Stand and Deliver. Stroud: The History Press

Cooknell, J. Some random recollections of life in a village in the early years of the present century

Evans, G. 2019. The Battle of Edgcote 1469. Northamptonshire Battlefields Society

Hollins, D. The Culworth Gang, article on Culworth village website

Gould, J. The Culworth Gang. Northamptonshire Past and Present 2000 no. 53

Hatmaker, DJ. 2021. Uneasy Heads. Corby: 3P Publishing

Mozley, T. 1885. Reminiscences, chiefly of Towns, Villages and Schools. Longmans Green and Co.

Poole, E. The story of Byfield. 1930

Newspaper cuttings from the weekly *Northampton Mercury*, the *Chronicle and Echo* and the *Northampton County Magazine.*

Author notes

I first became aware of a possible family connection with William Bowers of the Culworth gang whilst researching for my book *Highwaymen, Hangings and Heroes*. Enforced lockdown during the Coronavirus pandemic gave me the ideal opportunity to delve further into the antics of these eighteenth-century highwaymen and robbers. The closure of libraries and record offices limited available avenues of research, although many other sources, and interested local people, helped with the quest. I hope their details are correctly recorded in the appendix. This book succeeds a joint article which appeared in the Cogenhoe and Whiston Heritage Magazine, spread over three editions, December 2020 to February 2021, which I wrote with the help of the magazine's researcher Robert Vaughan. This book includes much additional material which came to light following the publication of the magazine article. In particular I was fascinated to learn that two Thornton girls, Jane and Elizabeth, were bridesmaids at the Culworth weddings of gang member William Pettifer/Peckover, suggesting the historic connection between several Northamptonshire families with which I appear to have a connection is possibly closer than previously realised.

Also by Richard Blacklee

Highwaymen, Hangings and Heroes

A Race for Wealth

Available from https://bookshop.3ppublishing.co.uk/

and from Amazon